"Where does a lively and still curious mind turn during these days of stultifying mundanity stripped of all but its utility? *The Words We Do Not Have* offers its certain refuge. With the deft turn of a phrase, observing where others are content to only see, setting aside the over-wrought histrionics that consumes so much current poetry, Steve Brisendine invites us along with him on an amble through streets and ideas not only engaging, but ultimately, in the deepest sense, rewarding."

-Will Leathem, Prospero's Books, Spartan Press

In The Words We Do Not Have, Steve Brisendine brings experience into sharp focus—a road trip with his son, evenings spent playing pool, an abused childhood classmate—along with meditative explorations of life, death, aging, and faith. The author employs as a title for each poem an unusual foreign word (along with its definition), a strategy that unifies the collection, while also yielding delightful and unexpected trajectories as the poems unfold. Brisendine's imaginative lexicon offers us a space where "a heart has/ spilled itself, where words bloomed/ into something past words."

-Janice Northerns, author of *Some Electric Hum*

"We have enough wind in Kansas," Steve Brisendine opens his excellent new book. "When you / walk into it, it pulls." Beginning with the language of wind, Brisendine reveals a dark world through a series of tongues. In "Mokita," a classmate is abused and silent, eventually dead. We learn the title's Kilivila meaning: "something everyone knows but no one talks about." Outlining a "slippery downhill way," these grave, sometimes minutial poems (as in "Qarba," the appearance of white hairs in a man's beard) highlight how life gives us "hope of reunion . . . but also the knowledge that such might never happen." Dark, global, nuanced in how it reveals a gritty world."

>-Tyler Robert Sheldon, Editor-in-Chief of
>*MockingHeart Review* and author of *Consolation Prize* (Finishing Line Press, 2018)

The Words We
Do Not Have

Poems by Steve Brisendine

Kansas City   Missouri

Spartan Press
Kansas City, MO
spartanpress.com

Copyright © Steve Brisendine, 2021
First Edition: 1 3 5 7 9 10 8 6 4 2
ISBN: 978-1-952411-52-6
LCCN: 2021931849

Cover image: Jon Lee Grafton
Author photo: Alan Hainkel
All rights reserved. No part of this publication may be reproduced or transmitted in any form or by any means, electronic or mechanical, including photocopying, recording or by info retrieval system, without prior written permission from the author.

Acknowledgments:

Wow … where do I start here? I suppose that has to be with my mother, Geraldine, who sat me up in a kitchen chair when I was three years old and started teaching me to read. That began a love of words and wordplay that has lasted until now and likely will endure as long as I do.

My father, Charles, was a banker with the soul of a writer. He encouraged every creative outlet I pursued (okay, except for letting me try out the electric guitar in my teens, which was probably for the best) and taught me that men don't have to suppress the things we feel.

My wife, Kerri, has indulged my poetry habit over the years and has a gift for catching the things that don't quite work and need to be fixed. Both of those things are appreciated more than words can convey.

My late sister, Cynthia Romito, saved my life twice. "Saudade," this book's final piece, is the last thing I read to her in the hospice and is dedicated to her memory.

I am beyond indebted to the talented poets I know and have known, who shared their own work and encouraged mine – especially the poets of Prospero's Pit and of the Friday night events at Allen Heinrich's place – and to the editors who, over the years, published the efforts of former alter ego Stephen Clay Dearborn.

It would take forever to name all of the people in either category (many are in both) but there are three I would like to single out. Allen, a true lover of poetry and a gracious host to those who share that love – is one. Will Leathem – friend, raconteur, publisher, facilitator of those

Pit sessions on 39th Street – is another. I also want to thank Shawn Pavey, whose input and encouragement over the course of this project have given me even more reason to be grateful for his friendship.

I have never met Adam Jacot de Boinod, but I am in his debt. His book, *The Meaning of Tingo and Other Extraordinary Words from Around the World,* inspired this project and provided me with so much material.

To those of you who suggested words for the book, thank you. To those who inspired poems – even if you never knew it – thank you. To those who read my drafts and offered your kind thoughts, thank you. And to you who now hold this book in your hand, thank you for giving these poems your time.

-Steve Brisendine, February 2021

The Words We
Do Not Have

TABLE OF CONTENTS

Foreword by Shawn Pavey

Uitwaiien / 1

Yúyīn / 6

Torschlusspanik / 8

Mokita / 11

Riman / 13

Badkruka / 14

Eno / 16

Eigengrau / 18

Emakou / 21

Madrugada / 23

Dolilyts / 24

Tarere / 27

Qiangda / 29

Jeitinho / 30

Qarba / 34

Piropo / 36

Wabi-Sabi / 38

Saruz-ram / 41

Labrish / 42

Ayurnamat / 45

Tretår / 47

Samir / 49

Tsundoku / 51

Efterarsfarver / 53

Dizlanmak / 56

Adjal / 58

Saudade / 60

Foreword by Shawn Pavey

I've known Steve Brisendine for almost as long as I've been in Kansas City. I moved here to pursue a relationship that started falling apart about the minute I rolled into town. The only reason I mention this is because there I was, completely alone in a town where the only person I knew wanted very little to do with me, but I had a good job and a good feeling about the place. So, I went out to find some like-minded folks.

I discovered The Writers Place, a literary non-profit that used to reside in an old stone castle-looking building in Midtown. There, I met Will Leathem, proprietor of Prospero's Books and, at the time, Executive Director of TWP. He introduced me to a group of performance poets led by Allen Heinrich who hosted regular gatherings in his apartment to recite and perform poetry. This is where I met Steve.

Since then, he's been there through a couple of bad breakups, he was present when my wife and I had our first date, we bought a house in Mission, KS two and a half blocks from Steve's house (it was a happy accident, but still), he helped me celebrate my wedding, and has helped me polish off copious quantities of various and sundry spirits, usually around some semblance of an open flame on the verge of becoming a catastrophe.

A few years back, Steve shared this manuscript and it floored me. A book of poems about words, sure. We've seen that. Poems about words in other languages that do not translate to English, more rare. But an entire collection? I've never seen that.

Steve Brisendine's poems in *The Words We Do Not Have* echo in the brain pan and the breadbasket long after putting them down. He speaks in raw, honest, beautifully written language about those very real states of being for which we have no English. Using words pulled from a myriad of human tongues about, for instance, *Uitwaaien*, from the Dutch: To walk in the wind, for enjoyment or to clear one's head from the pressures of life. Or *Mokita,* from Kilivila in Papua New Guinea: Something everyone knows but no one talks about.

These fine poems border on confessional but not in the most conventional sense. While Ginsberg and Whitman may howl and yawp in the background of this work, Brisendine, by revealing and sharing his personal experience, sheds light on the holy universality of all human existence as we walk the earth under a wide blue sky.

Shawn Pavey
Mission, KS
March 30th, 2021

For the Teacher, whoever he was

There are doubtless many different languages in the world, and none is without meaning.

-1 Corinthians 14:10 (ESV)

Uitwaaien

Dutch: To walk in the wind,
for enjoyment or to clear one's
head from the pressures of life.

> *Don't hang on;*
> *nothing lasts forever*
> *but the earth and sky*
> -Kerry Livgren

I.

We have wind enough in Kansas.
        This is not the issue.

But time alone, idle
time, time and times
on the far side of again –

how far do you have to
walk to wear out ghosts
        of starved nights

and smothered
        declarations?

*(There is more I meant
to say here, but the
branches have stopped
moving and it is too
quiet to think)*

II.

If these tulips would
hold still, I could
        send you their picture.

The tall one is boisterous,
whipping back and
forth; it calls your name,
        misspelled, and grins.

I do not know
what sort of bribe to offer
        for good behavior.

III.

I was fourteen, or just shy of,
the day red Permian dirt
        howled in from the south.

A mile home from the
junior high school, give
or take, the right side of my

face stinging; fingers can
        stop only so much.

It came in under a back
door, spread itself across
the kitchen floor and
infiltrated cats' fur,
dared us to roll up rugs
and fight back with
        brooms and wet towels.

As children of the Dust
Bowl, my parents shrugged
and let old muscle
        memories take over.

        I'd come in so coated,
my father said,
        that you couldn't tell if I was black
        or white.

Wind knows all our
exhaled stories, and how
        they end. Earth

(the LORD God called the man

        Adam,

which means

        red dirt)

is our shared epilogue,
the blanket of sleepers
waiting for the last
> morning of the world.

>*I coated the feet of things
>that died so dinosaurs
>could move in,*

driven dust
hissed through the big elm
in our back yard.

>*I can wait.*

IV.

The darkness that waits
between streetlights has
> always been here.

It remembers long grass.

It strains against glows
that push it back. When you
walk into it, it pulls. When
you walk out of it,
> it pulls.

It wants stars back, silences
> of nights with no wind.

Patience,

I say, and step into
      another pool of light.

      Patience. We will not always
          be here.

Yúyīn

Chinese: a sound which lingers in the ears of the hearer.

My father meant only to distract me
with an errand, a needless trip to
        Chaffin Hardware, where the owner

(who, like almost everyone else in our
little town, knew my mother's time was
down to hours or minutes, and so treated me
        with solemn concern in hushed tones)

made me a duplicate ignition key for
        the station wagon.

My father's instinct was, as mine would be,
to get me away, to insulate me from that
        moment when her chest fell, fluttered

        (perhaps; I was not there)

and did not rise again. In this, he achieved
        his aim; she was gone when I returned.

He could not have known, and I never told
        him (and cannot now),

that the gritty metallic whine of a blank

being ground into functionality would always
unlock well-used doors behind which
    regret waits sleepless.

Torschlusspanik

*German: The anxiety caused by the
realization that time is passing and
opportunities are diminishing.
Literally, "panic at the closing of the gate."*

> *In which Janus, God of Doorways,
> orders another round:*

Every year, same thing: People
      crowding through at midnight,

half of them two glasses past stupid, and
of course they can't be bothered
      to shed their excess baggage.

Then they all get cranky with me
      for not telling them,

      Hey, don't bring that in here
or not asking,
      *Are you sure you didn't forget
      anything?*

And man, do I get tired of hearing
all those biological time bombs ticking –
for men, too, but their sound is
more like a comb dragging hair across
      a bare scalp, over and over.

Nothing I can do; the rules say I have
to let people through with whatever
> they can manage to carry.

Regulations. I don't search. I don't seize.
> I open the way, that's all.

I didn't even build the gate in the
first place; one day is the same as
another to me, and I stopped counting
> years when Rome fell.

Pay's decent, though, and aside
from one night, the schedule's
> pretty light.

I wish they'd shut up and keep the
line moving, though; all this talk
of plans and resolutions, when I
> heard the same thing last year.

See, they get through, and the
scenery hasn't changed, and neither
have they, and they want to blame
> me for that, too.

Not my job. Not my problem. And
besides, I'm either on break or off
duty, whichever will get me left
> in the most peace.

Anyone with complaints between now
and the end of next December can take
          them up with the Fates, or Fortuna.

Gimme another. Better make it a double,
but put it in two glasses, just in case
          last year's face wakes up.

Mokita

Kilivila (Papua New Guinea): Something everyone knows but no one talks about.

Mostly, his shirts covered the worst of it --
but sometimes, he'd come to school on
a short-sleeve day with

                 Don't-ask

  marks peeking out.

The new kids all learned pretty
quickly, after the first wince and gasp,
        not to slap him on the back.

We knew the difference between clumsy
and buckle, but laws and codes (both
written and quietly understood) were
        different then.

                If you see something,
                    say nothing.

Some guys just had it rough like that,
and there was always a chance he'd
get worse than welts
        if a charge didn't stick.

So we had him spend the night when we
could, or stayed at his place when things
were relatively safe there: haven on
one hand, a reason for restraint in
> front of witnesses on the other.

Even then, we cut our eyes sideways and
down when his dad was in the room, and
> we always made sure to say

> *Sir.*

He is dead now, or I would not be telling
any of this. I do not know the how, and have
> not looked hard for it.

I have apologized to his headstone, more
> than once. No answer ever comes.

Riman

*Arabic: The sound a stone makes
when it is thrown at a boy.*

I was seven when I pegged Stan Sherwood
        with a rock for no offense that I can recall;

he was quiet, and not one to start trouble,
though I do remember that I envied him
        for having better crayons.

The words of the apology my father made me
        write to him

(using my basic sixteen-count
        box of Crayolas)

are lost to me – but I cannot forget that dull crack
        of impact against his head

(he wore his hair close-cropped,
what we called a
                Butch;

there was no cushion against a
        stone's full force),

or the slow raising of his hand to the struck spot,
eyes wide behind wire-rimmed glasses, asking me
        a question to which I still have no answer.

Badkruka

*Swedish: "Bath coward," one reluctant to get
into the water when swimming outside.*

So I never learned to swim,
in that hot windy week
of a scrubby Texas summer
when I was eleven,
        and nervous.

I trembled on the dock, huddled
into myself, waiting my turn;
when it came, I shook
                No,
resigned to five days alone
        with crafts and jeers

(the closest camp companions
of a childhood largely spent
        wandering in my own head).

Then again, I missed out on
feeding leeches that fattened
        themselves on half my troop,

and I have since learned to swim –
though now, I worry less about water
closing over me, and more about it

coming in through that crack
        in the foundation.

I am fifty-three,
        and nervous.

Eno

Finnish: Maternal uncle.

Chet Ashlock looked like old pictures
of my grandfather, had that same
        high reedy voice.

I met him twice,
never heard him sing.

Once, when I was
        (I think) five,

he brought along his family. They, too,
are as lost to me as the ash tree that stood
        in my old front yard,

or photographs ruined
        by water.

He was occasional to an extreme,
at most an
                I remember
but more often a passing
                I wonder

When my mother died,
        he sent vague regrets.

I have no idea when he followed her.
If I mourn
      (which is seldom),

it is most often with a shrug –
not for one I miss,
      but for what was missed.

Sometimes, though,
the wondering goes sharp,
      turns on end,

finds a space between ribs,
      jabs itself in deep.

Eigengrau

*German: Grey in its purest state; the deep grey
seen by the eyes in the absence of light.*

I worked in darkrooms, back before ones
        and zeroes took over.

High school yearbook, hometown newspaper,
a half-improvised setup in my own basement –
        the routine is still fresh:

a careful pop of the canister;

        *(Don't bend the lid;
        you'll need it for your next roll)*

taking off the film leader with one practiced cut,
        scissors returned to place;

that quick back-and-forth ratchet of moving film
        from roll to reel;

another cut, to free film
        from spool;

        *(Don't pull the tape;
        might be static, and sparks
        will fog the negatives)*

one delicate stroke with the right thumbnail, to make
>   sure everything lines up;

reaching ahead and to the right to grab the top
>   to the developing tank.

(It was always there. I did not need to fumble.
>   Muscles remember.)

To say
>   *I could do it with my eyes closed*

was less cliché than necessity.

I kept them squeezed tight, pressure enough
>   to fire optic nerves.

They showed me illusions: sudden auroras, clouds
ringing transient stars, streaks of a shade just shy of grey
>   raining from upper left to lower right.

Once, I left them open for ten seconds. That was as
>   long as I could endure.

Something intangible came out of the blackness,
>   struck me with a thought:

> > *This is the view of the blind,*
> > *this flat and boundless*
> > *expanse of not-anything.*

My eyelids slammed shut on knowledge. White
        spots flared and receded.

One deep breath. Another. Then I screwed on the lid,
flicked a switch, blinked hard, glad for
        a sting of light.

Emakou

Gilbertese: A sadness kept hidden from the world.

When you build labyrinth walls
        with words

but can't remember where you put
        gateways,

everything begins to turn in
        on itself:

spirals of allusion, blind alleys
        of double meaning,

        (This way leads nowhere, but
            it is broad and well-lit)

and eventually the string
        runs out.

Oh, you can try sending up something
        bright and blazing,

but by the time they figure out just what
you mean by red doors and green
        eyes and –

Wait, I have not written
that one yet, outside of dreams –

you're dry and grinning at the last thing
you scratched into stone;

that, or you meet the thing at the heart
of the maze,

hear it breathe your metaphors and clatter
clatter your careful cadences from three
turns of phrase and passage away.

Face it.

See that scar on its lip,
another on its forehead,
two crooked fingers.

Put out your hand;
find cool mirrored glass.

Realize that no one
is coming.

Madrugada

*Spanish/Portuguese: The time
between midnight and 4 a.m.*

Come on out under streetlights.
Pace barefoot on asphalt; feel
it rasp the balls of your feet with
        every step, a burn when you lift.

Streets want to sleep, too – but
how can they, with you dragging
voweled petitions up from
        your dry pinched throat?

Someone calls these
        the wee small hours,

you know they never went in
and out of a front door, trying to
        keep that bad hinge from squealing.

        Let this cup pass,

you breathe with night air at
your back – then turn away into
        darkness and add,

        or pour me a double and be done.

Dolilyts

*Ukrainian: To lie with one's face
turned to the ground.*

Explain this to me:

How can You make a man a chew toy
        for a disgraced and sociopathic cherub,

let that man beat the ground where
his children bled out and beg
        You for even half of a why,

and then drive up in a tornado,
answering grief with a sarcastic

        Where were you when …?

If this is Love, and we are told that
You are, we know well that care and
kindness sometimes must wield clean
sharp steel to dig out splinters, apply
a scream of hot iron to a bleeding stump
(over pleas of

        Please, no),

        pump in poison to kill cancer.

But forgive us if we fear to sing a
new song, lest we be ordered to hold
that final wide-open vowel of an

> *Alleluia*

so You can knock out
        an abcessed molar –

and yet I have known graces given,
held tight to lines of mercy that drew
me up from my hand-dug abysses
        and set me on new (again) footing.

I cannot reconcile.

The columns match and balance, and
yet I am unable to make them agree;
paradox is the sum of itself. I must
        solve for doubt.

You say

        Come, let us reason …

and I say

        Make this make sense,

and you say

        Be still and know.

This is why we cannot be allowed
        to grasp the ways of God in full:

Either we become a race prone in the dirt,
eyes mudding our ancestral and eventual
dirt, coughing out racked cries of

> *Unclean ...*

with all remaining breaths – or we go mad,
chuck the bones of our dead into the whirlwind,
        curse and die.

Love, you say?

Tastes like blood and dust to me.

> *Now,*

You reply in a voice like the clank and
ring of a mallet on a spike. Wind changes,
        and I smell linen and grave-spices.

> *Now you begin*
> *to take hold.*

Tarere

*Cook Islands Maori: The act of sending
another flying through the air.*

> *In which Athena, Goddess of Wisdom,
> goes to the batting cages ...*

There's only so much idiocy she can
take before her own brow splits open just
      like Daddy's.

It's either this, or loosing owls to see
how folly likes a faceful of talons; the
      workout wins.

She's in a groove, shoulders loose, smooth
level swings at every buffoon the machine
      throws her way:

conspiratorial screwballs, easily swayed
sliders, nasty cutters of a thousand
      comment sections.

She spit-chants a cadence of sweet-spot
      contact:

> *Your, you're;
> there, their, they're;
> to, too, two.*

Feels good. Feels right. She puffs a stray
curl away from one cool grey eye, adjusts
        her helmet –

and then some mashed-up knuckleball
comes to, shakes his head, half-mumbles

              great again.

Artemis has been watching, when she's
not setting dogs on anyone she sees
        eying her legs.

> *You can't knock any sense into them,*
> *you know,*

she says in that moonbeam drawl,

> *and I'm bored.*

> *Come on; there's a herd of pundits down*
> *by the lake. I brought an extra bow and*
> *quiver for you.*

> *They don't stay down any longer than*
> *this bunch, or learn any better, but I like*
> *hearing them yelp.*

Qiangda

Mandarin: To race to be the first to answer a question.

Here is your tiebreaker:

Using a stolen pencil with the eraser end chewed off,
write down your answer to the following question and
       bring it to the scorer's table.

You have forty-five seconds,
       give or take your average lifespan.

All answers are final, except for the one given out
       five minutes before everyone got here.

Winners will be announced at some point,
or perhaps not. You do not have to be present
       to win, but you will lose face if you are absent.

Here is the question:

> *What is the name given to the fear
> of unfinished or incomplete*

Jeitinho

Brazilian Portuguese: The "little way" of getting what one wants through unofficial channels; finding a way around.

There is nothing new under
        the table, son.

The road through all bureaucratic hells
        is paved with stony refusal –

a slick and unforgiving surface,
suitable for labyrinths, for
        cul-de-sacs and blind alleys –

but traction can be (and so often is)
gained by transaction, and footing found
        on greased skids.

                Surely,
one side says,
                we can come
                to an agreement –

And here is that pause, for
consideration of proper
        considerations.

Value, values: Negotiations
are open. Price and worth are
both in play, and accommodations
are available now and beyond
        the hours of our deaths.

Greeks put coins in the mouths
of corpses, so they could pay boat fare
        across the Styx into Hades.

From entry to escape: one of
ninety-five things that made
        Martin Luther nailing mad

was the sale of indulgences:
in essence (and with plenty of incense),
cards to get out of Purgatory early –
        but not, of course, free.

Times change; people do not.
I have seen men and women on
pay-as-you-go television, flashing
        five-figure smiles

(dragons'-teeth veneers are pricey,
yes, but look at how they gleam)
        and assure the faithful of two things:

that the well-connected shall inherit
both Here and After, and that

  even figurative silver makes an
      excellent conductor.

Call now; lines are open. Pay
    no heed to hooks.

There is no remission without remittance,
the shedding of goods at well-shod feet,
and how great is the art
    of a well-struck deal.

Let us join hands, with a little
something passing from one to
    the other, and sing praises.

I am not convinced, though, that it is
possible to cross a palm with anything
    persuasive, when

the outstretched hand in question
has felt the bite of base metal,
a brutal fastening to wood on
    a bloody Friday afternoon.

Drop one coin, or thirty; they will
all fall through nail-holes into
    pathless dark.

You do not want to know where
they land, or to follow them along

      that slippery downhill way.

Not all accommodations offer
peaceful rest,
      or any at all.

Qarba

Persian: The appearance of white hairs in a man's beard.

Sure, it throws you – that first thick, wiry,
kinked-up reminder that the target demographic
        stayed behind, and you moved on.

And no, it wasn't always like this – the worship
of unlined faces, taut frame, hairless
        everything but heads –

but things change, and they're not going to change
        back just to suit you.

No point in trying to color facts out of existence,
my friend; dye never softened anything, especially
        not a come-along smack from time.

Only so many you can pull, too – maybe one
or two at a time, but no more; sore and patchy
        isn't a good look on anyone, man.

You could break out a razor and try to shave a
couple of years off the guesses, maybe hear
                Sir
        less often in grocery checkout lines,

or stave off being asked

Would you like to see
the senior menu?

for a bit longer; it's not as though you would be
        the only one taking that backpedal road.

But how can you show off your other scars, tell
the stories behind them, and not embrace those
you got from being attacked by clocks and calendars,
        year upon decade?

Look at you, still going despite free will and
brain chemistry and triple-barreled scattershots
        of time and chance and family histories.

(This is my morning speech to my mirror; someday,
        someday, my reflection will nod
              You're right.)

Piropo

Argentinean Spanish: A compliment paid to
a woman encountered in public; not the same
as a catcall, though some can be quite bold.

The equations laid out before
you are diamonds to my
        graphite brain;

sharpen it though I might on
the finely gritty grids of this
crossword puzzle, I cannot
        penetrate those mysteries.

I am more concerned with
properties of wavelength
and reflection, words
and symbols one might employ
        to encompass them,

        (Let no one argue
        against the existence
        of oak-colored light,
        for your eyes are luminous)

and the simple physics which
        govern lines of sight.

(When I lean back,
I can meet your gaze,
and so I will lean back)

Wabi-Sabi

*Japanese: A deep appreciation of the beauty of
transience, assymetry and imperfection.*

This is a message
found in a bottle, floating
in an ancient pond:

five
seven
five

rigid
five; sevenfive
       or fiveseven; five –

Haiku 101 with
Professor Procrustes,
who will tell you to stretch
or amputate so the verse
       fits unforgiving form;

stop.

Exhale once and then
       breathe this in:

Fingers are for sifting
ashes and cemetery dirt, not
      reckoning ruled syllables.

Think in threes, yes, and
      in a sequence of

five (ELEGY)
seven (REQUIEM)
      five (DIRGE) --

stop.

One breath in again,
one breath out
      again.

This is the time you have
to take in the life of a moment,
the time you have to
      speak its death.

All haiku are translated from
Tralfamadorian –
infinite permutations of
      So it goes,

Spoken over that which has passed
      and cannot return.

Do you doubt? Crown yourself a second
        Canute, then.

Take your seat where time's waves break
        and order reversals:

dead leaf back to branch,
ripples into still center,
        imago withdrawn into chrysalis --

stop.

Your feet are wet.
Walk them dry, eyes open to
brief beauties of a world
        of endings without end,

and in the span of a frog's leap,
let all the people breathe
        Entropy, amen,

and set a watch on new graves;
        grass will return.

Saruz-ram

*Persian: The breaking of the day's first light
upon one devoted to a life of contemplation.*

The sunlight is gaunt,
air sharp around
its edges, minutes in
       both all too brief;

all the same, I breathe
       in and out a litany of

              thanks be

(though not in so many
sounds; this is a silent
Hour of Prime, by
       time if not by name)

              let all be a Psalm,
              a Song of Ascents;
              sing you birds and
              winter-thin squirrels

Labrish

*Jamaican Patois: Good-natured gossip
and joking, mixed in with songs and
recollections of school days.*

It was 1984, and we were grandmasters
of Hoodoo in the corner pocket, deans
of the Hidden College of Eight-ball,
        whileaway brothers of Phi Kappa Tau.

We spent our study hours calculating
double-bank shots and honing our command
        of breaks and bending English.

Still, science could only take us so far;
beyond borders of the known, where
long shots to northeast corners always
        shear left,

and anything into the bumper closest to
the stairs died faster than a six-pack
when the Chiefs were on, and you had to drink
        every time the call was

        Billy Jackson up the middle
(throw in
        No gain,

and you had to down a whole can at once),

there was – and perhaps still is, for those who
can find a true and crooked path to it –
      the Realm of Hexovoodoo.

They mined for Woofledust there, ground it
to invisibility and shipped it out by misspent
night to those who knew just how and when
to sprinkle a handful in front of the other guy's
straight-on shot, so it caromed off and maybe
      he scratched to boot.

You couldn't use it too liberally, though, or
he'd build up an immunity and you'd be
      the one buying pitchers at Kite's.

Those true adepts among us –

and I'm not bragging, but I could hang with Steve
and his real brother Rat, with Fudge and Goetz
and Frank, Rossker and both Porches –

      knew where real power lay.

Shape and move your hands just right, say
the words and mean them, and it was just like
      weaving steel webs in front of pockets.

Nothing could get through Evil Bats,
Humping Frogs, the mystic sign of

      Tyrannosaurus rex –

not unless you knew countercharms, and
        even then, things could get dicey.

There was only one that worked, no matter what
anyone might have told you. My guess is that it
still holds all of its power -- and if you don't
know it, don't look at me to initiate you
        into the Order.

You think the handshake is a deep secret?
It's got nothing on handshapes that
just might keep you from losing control
        of the table.

> *What principles do we hold dear,*
> *my brothers?*

> *Not to be low-rent,*
> *nor a vagrant, nor a wingnut,*
> *and not to speak against Van Halen.*

> *We ratify this*
> *with clack and clatter*
> *of ball, rack and cuestick.*

> *So mote it be.*

Ayurnamat

*Inuit: The philosophy that one should not worry
about things which one cannot change.*

Don't come knocking at my screen and my brain
        on a warm April evening,

asking if I have a minute to talk about
impact events, or overdue eruptions,
or the inevitability of the wrong monkey
        biting a traveler in Cameroon

and me bleeding out through the eyes
        three weeks later.

No, you may not come in. I've seen your kind at
work: Get in the door, try to keep me up all night
        obsessing over catastrophes and coverups.

I am aware that fault lines and tropical depressions
spawn monsters regardless of my wishes or anyone
        else's, that madmen have their hands on launch
codes,

and that if there are people with enough juice
to run the world from the shadows, I am not
one who can stop them – and besides that,
        my house is a mess.

Now, if you want to help me keep the lights on,
or you know how to get another ten thousand
miles out of a 17-year-old Toyota, then
        have a seat and let's talk.

At the very least, proofread a poem for me
and tell me whether that metaphor in line 38
        makes any sense outside my head.

These are the things that snap me awake at two a.m.
and set me pacing, listening to wind mutter
        in maple branches.

No, it's fine. I had no expectations. Your
        alarm trumpet sounded impressive, though.

You have a great night now, and watch out
        for whatever frightens you most.

I won't wait up.

Tretår

Swedish: The second refill of a cup of coffee.

The third cup of coffee likes you.

The third cup of coffee finds you
        fascinating, in fact.

The third cup of coffee can't wait to hear
your poetry, or the idea behind the novel
        that you start every November,

the one where all your dead relatives –
or the main character's dead relatives,
        but they say *Write what you know* –

come back every autumn between
the fall of the first leaf and the fall
        of the first snowflake.

The third cup of coffee is impressed that you
        have never lost to a Sunday crossword,
        and that you are trying to write one yourself.

        You have to think diagonally, because
        words have so many definitions,

you say, and the third cup of coffee nods hard
        because it knows just what you mean.

The third cup of coffee wants to know what
you did last weekend, and what your plans are
      for tonight, and whether you think

Spain and Catalonia and the Basque Country
(the third cup of coffee understands, and raises
both eyebrows in appropriate appreciation,
when you call it

            Euskadi)

      should shake hands and go their separate ways.

And then it's gone, and every eye in the place
      is glazed and cold as your mug,

and there is no one else
      at the table.

Samir

Persian: One who converses at night by moonlight

This is how stories begin, half-hushed
firelight tales of a beautiful passenger who
        is there, and then (in an instant) is not.

She ghosted from the back seats of the westbound 39
on a warm fall evening, all white skin and shadowed
persimmon hair (I heard no footsteps behind me
        or even at my side until she spoke).

She asked about the 107, and I did not know;
there was a subsoft murmur under her breath,
        something sounding like

home,

and then she looked ahead and said no more, though
        we kept pace side by side.

She turned at Rainbow, the gleam and shimmer of her
        outshining streetlights and moon beyond;

I looked away – not for long – and all who have
        sat in shadows of trees,

what-was-that
sounds just behind them,

will know what I saw, and who I did not,
when I looked back.

Tsundoku

*Japanese: The practice of buying a book
and then leaving it unread, usually stacked
with other unread books.*

> *Never enough time to read
> all that I want,*

the chant of an aging reader

    drones on
        *(excuse without end,
        amen)*

and still I keep volumes of
once-wanted writings

    waiting

(somewhat neatly, by category;
small semblances of order
must be maintained, even
when life sits stacked in a tidy

    shambles),

each new vague promise piled
upon a good intention, until

something gives way, the
shelf tumbles, and leaves

        scatter.

Efterarsfarver

Danish: The colors of autumn.

They met on the eve of the equinox.

                        Climb with me,
she said, and shapeshifted, becoming
a child and then a cat as she rose
        through branches.

Her eyes stayed blue, the color of
        September twilight.

He uprooted himself and followed,
        wooden joints creaking.

She laughed and prowled the tree,
transforming now and then back
        to her true shape.

                I haven't climbed in years,
he said.

                      Come up higher,

she said, and became a bird
        with a black cap.

She plucked a berry from his lips,
and another grew in its place.

They talked of winter, and ground
        grew white beneath them.

They talked of spring, and flowers
        painted the earth.

They spoke of summer, and cicadas
        pulsed the world to sleep.

And yet the tree's leaves remained
        and did not turn, until they
        spoke of autumn.

Even then leaves did not fall,
        but ripened to gold.

They stayed there for a century or so,
she changing as moods took her and he
        slowly grafting himself to the trunk.

From time to time she nested in his hands,
        or stretched along his arm, and slept.

Seasons passed around them, and yet
        the tree remained golden.

And then, she became a child once more,
> for another brief moment.

She sang a new song, and they both took back
> their forms and returned to the world.

Her lips were berry-sweet, and his eyes were blue,
> and she was not so young nor he so old.

Dizlanmak

Turkish: Perpetually humming to oneself.

For me, it is always Tchaikovsky
(and of course, The Nutcracker),
but none of those earworms you
hear in radio spots around
        Christmas time;

give me the soaring, sad and sweet
resonance of the *Pas de Deux,*
        and I will be –

what?

Happy is not the true word, but
melancholy is too extreme in
        the other extreme.

Call it a blissful sorrow, or ache
with joy-streaks running through
        it, shining as silver

(or tears);

                Tchaikovsky never could
                write a decent transition,

my friend Gary says. He is smarter
than I, in nearly very other matter,

but here I say that he misses the point
          and the blood it draws.

Listen to the languid build, the brass
portending something glorious and
shattering, the whirling descent of
          that final passage,

and tell me there is no move from
a hesitant hope of

          maybe

into that
terrifying joy of

          yes,

a timestopping
    crash of

          now –

all shadowed by knowledge that
          This cannot last.

Pay no undue credence to any flourish
at the close; it is a brave face painted
          onto wet-eyed truth.

All dances end, in the end, and all who
dream love awaken either into this
          world or the next;

still, let an orchestra play on so long
as it will, even if notes sound only
          inside my own head.

Adjal

*Indonesian: The hour at which
a person is fated to die.*

> *In which we find Thanatos, God of Death,
> on 39th Street in Kansas City, Missouri:*

My Death –
by which I mean the particular Death
who carries my name
       in his appointment book –

finds himself at loose ends,
       having within the last hour dispatched

one gut-shot burglar,
two octogenarians,
and an entire carload
       of illegal immigrants.

His calendar is free until
3:27 tomorrow afternoon,
when he will oversee
the mauling of a CPA
       by two Akitas.

He wanders into Prospero's Books,
inquiring politely after a copy
       of Gorey's *The Unstrung Harp*,

settles instead for Thurber,
and nods politely on his way out
to a woman he will kill
with a 2002 Lincoln Town Car
        in a clearly marked crosswalk.

(My Death is unfailingly civil,
even when wielding
tornadoes,
saltwater crocodiles,
        pyroclastic clouds.)

My Death turns up the collar
on his black denim jacket.
He crosses the street to Blue Koi
to pick up an order
        of ginger basil chicken.

He does not take off his sunglasses,
        because my Death is cool.

In the evening, he will read this poem
        while he listens to "Ring of Fire"

and he will wish once more
that he could have traded me
        for Johnny Cash.

Saudade

Portuguese: The love and longing that remains, for a relationship or a time or a place that is lost. There is an implied hope of reunion or restoration, but also the knowledge that such might never happen.

--

If we never meet again,
if goodbyes remain unspoken,
I won't glorify our past,
but our bond remains unbroken
-Jules Shear

I.

I once had a book,
(one that did not go unread)
full of mixtape playlists
and recollections of loves begun,
       lived and –

can one really say

              ended?

Perhaps, but more precise to say

              changed

or

       shifted
or
       transformed;

love, like all things
  that matter,

is like matter. Once
it exists, it cannot be
  unmade –

converted to energy, yes, and
that with potential for
either/both creation and/or
  destruction beyond

words and medley, minor
  chords and key changes –

never brought to annihilation,
even when that would be a
  greater mercy;

life endures (if perhaps shadowed);
and so each song goes on, and our
stories with it, even decades after
  chapters close.

Dedication lines are always
open, even when no one
answers, and the hold music
  is enough to make you cry.

II.

> *Northbound on Interstate 35,*
> *a March morning in Noble*
> *County, Oklahoma*

Seven-thirty, a suggestion of
        sun. The world is down to this:

two strips of grey, coming out
        of fog and going into fog,

and silhouettes of bare trees
(against more grey, featureless)
on either side as we roll north
        toward Kansas.

My son and my younger self
ride shotgun; I share this driver's
        seat with my father's ghost.

            Remember,

we say to ourselves, and the word
        is plea, question, benediction.

Those in the passenger seat are
silent, one lost in sleep and the
other in something yielding and
        impenetrable as mist.

Home is out there,
        ahead and behind.

III.

Ron lost his wife six months ago; he pours out his pain in
        blue notes and gentle counterlines on Live Jazz
Thursdays.

She was my best friend,

he says after the set, over pints and between talk of
        old gigs and his next record.

The hole is always
going to be there.

He writes a word – this word; sounds it out, three soft
syllables lingering around the table like ghosts who have
        finally remembered what they meant to say in life.

He folds the paper, tucks it into his shirt
        pocket, pats it once.

This could be a song,

he says;

        an instrumental.

What else could it be, and still mean what it must mean?
        There are words we do not have, this side of
eternity.

We are breath-brief, frail and meant to sleep in dirt
from which we were drawn; we will arrive there
      soon enough.

For now, we make do; we raise imperfect Alleluias,
roar our rages, cry out soundshapes of longing, and
      hope for translation.

IV.

No land
where a heart has
spilled itself, where words bloomed
into something past words, truly
lies waste;

where love
returns to earth, flowers scented
with salt and soap will sprout
to show where it
once lived.

Steve Brisendine is a freelance writer, recovering journalist, poet and occasional artist based in Mission, Kansas. Under his former pen name of Stephen Clay Dearborn, his poetry has appeared in such publications as *Thorny Locust, Coal City Review, Potpourri, the Kansas City Star* and others. He was part of the Prospero's Pocket Poets series as Dearborn, but this is his first book under his own name.